THE SCOOP

ADRIANA LUNA CARLOS
Editor-In-Chief, Designer
and Co-Founder

HANNA OLIVAS
Managing Editor &
Co-Founder

ADVERTISING OPPORTUNITIES

Info@SheRisesStudios.com

THE SCOOP MAGAZINE
JULY 2025

SHE RISES
STUDIOS

CONTACT US

SheRisesStudios@gmail.com

WWW.SHERISESSTUDIOS.COM

LETTER FROM THE EDITORS

Dear Readers,

Welcome to the July 2025 edition of The Scoop Magazine, where we honor women who have taken the stage—and taken charge.

This issue, in partnership with the Her Bold Steps Summit (aired exclusively on FENIX TV), celebrates audacious visionaries who are rewriting the rules and reclaiming their narratives with unapologetic strength.

Gracing our cover is Brandi Liberty, a powerhouse leader and advocate whose work amplifies Indigenous voices with integrity and impact. As the CEO of The Luak Group, Brandi exemplifies what it means to lead from the heart while challenging systems not built for her people. Her story—rooted in heritage, resilience, and radical truth-telling—is a masterclass in fearless expression and transformative leadership.

In an era where self-expression is not just style, but power, we proudly spotlight the women who dare to show up as their full selves—boldly, beautifully, and without compromise. From cultural changemakers to fashion icons, this edition is packed with stories that inspire you to own your truth, speak louder, and step forward with no apologies.

Here's to the trailblazers, the storytellers, and the fierce women defining now.

Warm regards,

Adriana Luna Carlos & Hanna Olivas
Editors of The Scoop Magazine

Become a
Managing Partner

she wins
WOMEN'S NETWORK

Join a global Movement of Visionary Women
50+ Chapters. Transformative Community. Unlimited Growth.

WHAT'S INCLUDED

- 40% commission on memberships + event bonuses
- Leadership training, toolkits & ongoing support
- VIP access to retreats, masterminds & more

Join for just

www.shewinswomensnetwork.com

Application Fee (paid only after acceptance)

By Brandi Liberty

LEADING WITH HEART AND HERITAGE:

The Story of Brandi Liberty and The Luak Group

Brandi Liberty's journey is deeply rooted in the legacy of Indigenous resilience and leadership. An enrolled member of the Iowa Tribe of Kansas and Nebraska and a descendant of the United Houma Nation, Brandi embodies the spirit of service passed down by generations of strong Native women, especially her grandmother, who dedicated her life to helping their tribal community. For Brandi, leadership isn't just a role—it's a calling grounded in culture, community, and commitment.

Her path began over 16 years ago when she started writing grants for her tribe, initially viewing herself simply as someone trying to make a difference. *"I didn't think of myself as a CEO back then,"* she recalls. But with every project, every partnership, Brandi found herself building not just programs but the very infrastructure and sustainability that would empower Indigenous communities to thrive. From this work sprang The Luak Group, a unified platform combining decades of experience, cultural connection, and professional expertise to support Indian Country with Indigenous-led, culturally grounded, and technically sound solutions.

One of Brandi's earliest affirmations came in 2010 when she secured a $764,000 broadband infrastructure grant that brought fiber-to-the-premise internet to her reservation—transforming access to education, healthcare, and opportunity. *"Watching the shift from dial-up to broadband wasn't just a technical upgrade—it was about connecting our community to self-determination in a digital age."* Since then, her work has scaled to multi-million dollar housing projects, strategic planning, and national policy leadership.

Perhaps one of her most humbling moments was speaking at the National American Indian Housing Council's legal symposium, recognized alongside HUD leadership as a subject matter expert on tribal housing—a testament to years of dedication often unseen outside Indian Country.

Brandi's story is not without hardship. A survivor of narcissistic abuse, she faced years of manipulation and fear but emerged with renewed strength and purpose. Today, as Treasurer of the National Indigenous Women's Resource Center,

she channels her personal journey into advocacy for Native women and families, ensuring that voices like hers influence policy and change.

Securing over $135 million in federal and state grant awards for tribal projects is a milestone Brandi holds with deep significance. *"It's more than numbers—it's domestic violence programs, safe homes for elders, youth programming, and infrastructure where there was none."* Each dollar is a step toward honoring the sacrifices of Indigenous matriarchs before her and building a future where Native communities flourish on their own terms.

Yet balancing cultural integrity with federal systems remains a constant challenge. *"These systems were not created with Indigenous values in mind,"* she explains. Her role as a cultural translator involves advocating for flexibility and cultural accommodations, reminding funders that tribal decision-making often requires ceremonies, consensus, and time for healing. Brandi draws strength from her healing journey and refuses to let systems gaslight her or the communities she serves. *"I stand firm and offer alternatives that honor our protocols while meeting technical requirements."*

As a Native woman leader who grew up urban but remains deeply connected to her roots, Brandi has faced challenges of identity and belonging. She recounts a painful moment in graduate school when a classmate questioned her authenticity because she didn't grow up on a reservation. *"That moment taught me that authenticity isn't about fitting someone else's definition—it's about knowing who you are and refusing to apologize for it."* Today, she proudly leads from that place of authenticity, sharing her story through co-authoring Womanhood: Identity to Intimacy and Everything in Between and writing a forthcoming book focused on Native women in leadership.

"Leading with heart means never forgetting who I'm doing this work for," Brandi says. It means showing up with empathy, humility, and listening deeply to tribal communities—honoring their pace, history, and sovereignty. Inspired by her grandmother's example, she strives to protect her boundaries while advancing tribal visions of healing and self-determination. *"It's never performative. It's personal."*

Brandi's advocacy extends beyond consulting to Indigenous representation in fashion, media, and storytelling—spaces where Native voices have historically been marginalized or misrepresented. *"When I walk the runway wearing Indigenous designs, I'm representing generations of Native women who weren't given a platform,"* she shares. As a columnist for Verite News and a cultural advocate, Brandi's work ensures that Native stories are told authentically, offering mirrors for Indigenous women to see their full complexity and power.

Mentorship has been a cornerstone of Brandi's growth. Reflecting on her time at the Northern Ponca Housing Authority, she credits her mentor Joey Nathan for believing in her before she believed in herself—offering support that went beyond professional guidance into deep personal care. *"Joey changed my life,"* Brandi says. Today, she pays that forward, mentoring Indigenous women and leaders with honesty, empathy, and a commitment to lifting others as she climbs. *"Mentorship isn't transactional—it's relational."*

To young Indigenous professionals, especially women stepping into leadership or entrepreneurship, Brandi offers this advice: *"You are enough exactly as you are. Leadership starts the moment you trust your voice and act on your vision.*

Protect your peace. Set boundaries. Surround yourself with people who believe in you, and don't be afraid to take up space." She encourages embracing one's lived experience as a profound strength, not a limitation.

Looking ahead, Brandi's vision is clear and expansive. She is writing her second book centered on Native women leaders and serving as Senior Tribal Corporate Relations Executive for Nuweh LLC, focusing on intertribal economic development. She's exploring a Ph.D. to research trauma-informed, culturally responsive housing systems for survivors of domestic violence and abuse. Meanwhile, she continues to be a fierce voice for Indigenous rights and healing, using storytelling and advocacy to shift systems and empower communities.

Brandi Liberty's leadership is a tapestry woven from heritage, resilience, and relentless commitment. She leads with heart, honoring her ancestors while paving pathways for future generations.

In a world that often sidelines Indigenous voices, Brandi's story is a powerful reminder that authentic leadership rooted in culture and community is not only possible—it is transformative.

Connect With Brandi

THE LUAK GROUP
BRINGING SOLUTIONS TO INDIAN COUNTRY

www.theluakgroup.com
Instagram: @brandiliberty_

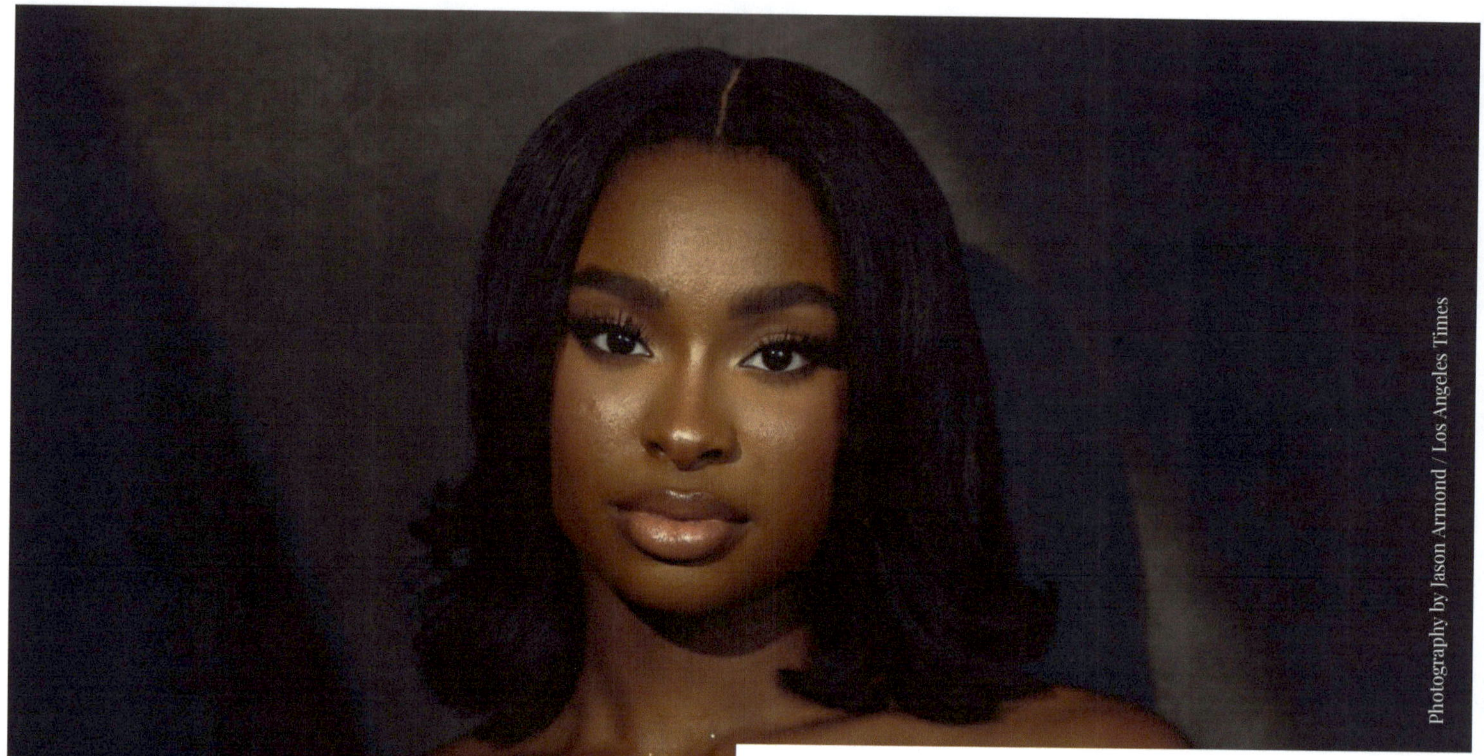

Photography by Jason Armond / Los Angeles Times

COCO JONES:

Rising Loud, Proud, and Unapologetically Herself

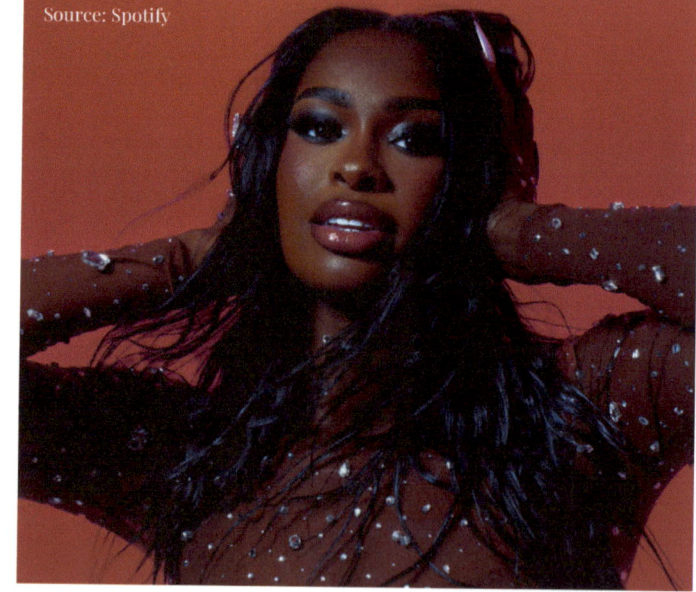

Source: Spotify

Coco Jones is not just having a moment—she's owning her era. With a voice that echoes strength and soul, and a presence that commands attention without ever begging for it, Coco is a modern icon of fearless expression. In a world that often tells young Black women to shrink, dilute, or mold themselves to fit an impossible standard, Coco does the opposite—she expands, glows, and speaks up with bold clarity.

This July, The Scoop shines a spotlight on Coco Jones in our Bold & Unapologetic issue, honoring artists who embody the essence of authenticity. Coco is the perfect fit. She doesn't just perform—she tells the truth. Whether she's on stage belting out emotionally rich lyrics or onscreen captivating audiences in Bel-Air, she carries her story with pride. She's not afraid to talk about the challenges behind the spotlight—the waiting, the rejection, the reintroduction.

And in doing so, she becomes a mirror for so many others navigating their own journey to visibility and self-acceptance.

Coco's rise wasn't handed to her on a silver platter. After an early start in the industry with her Disney Channel fame, many assumed she was on a straight shot to superstardom. But the reality was different. For years, she faced the brutal truth of an industry that often overlooks or sidelines talent that doesn't conform to narrow standards of beauty and marketability. Rather than fold or fade away, Coco chose to speak up—publicly sharing how colorism and typecasting limited her opportunities.

That honesty—raw, vulnerable, and brave—resonated far beyond Hollywood. It wasn't just about her career. It was about being a dark-skinned Black woman in an industry and culture that still struggles with fully embracing all shades of Black beauty.

Photography by Cindy Romero

Coco's truth became a rallying cry. Not bitter, but bold. Not performative, but deeply real. And in that moment, Coco Jones wasn't just an entertainer—she became a symbol of visibility, of being seen and heard without apology.

Her musical breakthrough came not just because of her talent—though that's undeniable—but because of her willingness to wait for the right moment and the right message. Her debut EP, What I Didn't Tell You, isn't just a collection of songs—it's a declaration. From themes of heartbreak to empowerment, every lyric carries emotional weight, echoing the journey of a woman reclaiming her narrative. And her smash single "ICU" didn't just top charts—it stopped people in their tracks. It reminded audiences that R&B isn't dead, and neither is depth.

What sets Coco apart is her balance of grace and grit. She shows up glam, yes—but she also shows up grounded. Her interviews feel like heart-to-hearts. Her performances feel like testimonies. She's equally at home in a red carpet gown as she is in sweats, talking mental health, self-worth, and the value of patience. In an era where curated perfection is the norm, Coco's willingness to show the messy, in-between parts is radical.

She's also proof that your time is your time. That no matter how many doors close, if you stay ready and stay true, the right ones will open—and when they do, you'll be ready to walk through them with your head held high. That's exactly what Coco is doing now.

In every sense, Coco Jones is living boldly. She's reclaiming her voice, her image, her power—and she's inviting others to do the same. She's not waiting to be crowned—she's building her own throne. Her journey is a reminder that true beauty is found in the brave, and true success belongs to those who refuse to shrink.

This isn't just Coco's comeback—it's her arrival. And she's here to stay. Loud. Proud. And unapologetically herself.

STEP INTO THE SPOTLIGHT AS A HOST ON FENIX TV!

Are you ready to amplify your message, inspire others, and be part of a groundbreaking network dedicated to empowering women worldwide? FENIX TV is your platform to shine as a host, share your expertise, and connect with a global audience.

WHY HOST ON FENIX TV?

- Reach a worldwide audience passionate about empowerment
- Showcase your voice, brand, and expertise
- Join a community of inspiring leaders and changemakers
- Be part of a network that uplifts and celebrates women

Whether you dream of leading a talk show, sharing powerful stories, or educating and inspiring others—FENIX TV is where your voice matters!

SECURE YOUR SPOT TODAY!

Contact us now at **info@fenixtv.app**

Learn more at **https://fenixtv.app**

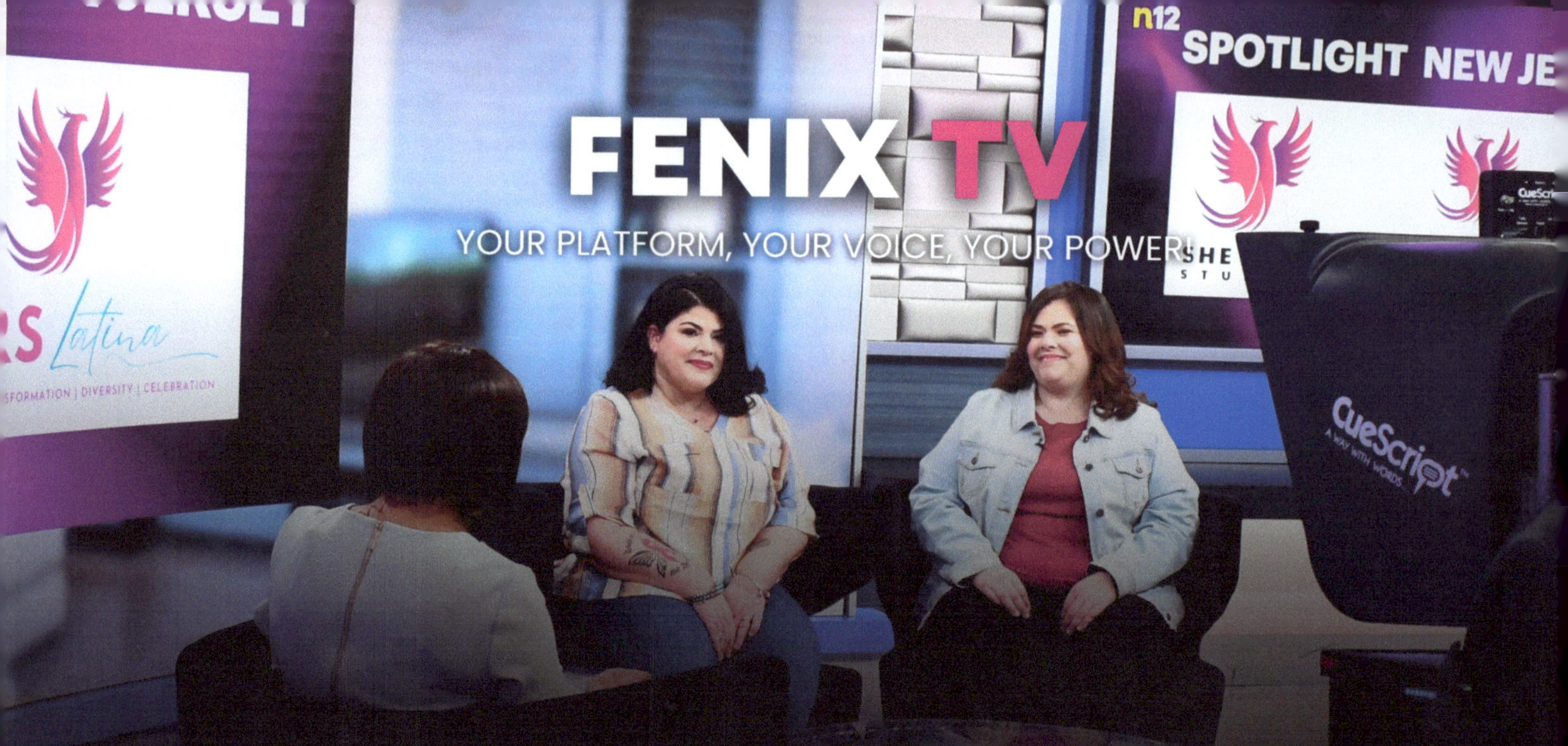

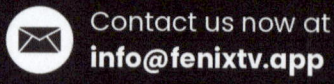

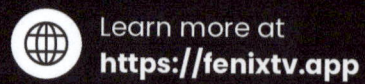

Empowering Women through Wellness and Self-Care

SHE
glows

HANNA OLIVAS

Along With 26 Inspiring Authors

SHOP NOW

GRAB YOUR COPY NOW

SHE GLOWS: Empowering Women Through Wellness and Self-Care is a radiant collection of stories and strategies from women who've made wellness a priority—and transformed their lives in the process. Through real experiences, expert insights, and practical tools, this empowering book shows how self-care is not selfish, but essential. From mindfulness and movement to nutrition and boundary-setting, these stories remind us that true glow comes from within. You are not alone—and these women prove that healing, balance, and joy are all within reach when you choose to care for yourself first.

amazon.com   **SHE RISES** STUDIOS

DON'T SHRINK
EXPAND

By DK Hillard

It happened again the other day. A powerful woman, someone you would never suspect harbored fear about who she was, walked through the door to my studio for our scheduled meeting. I had never met her in person so I was looking forward to sharing my work face to face. But in a very short period of time, as she interacted with my work, I felt the terror emanating from her body. She wasn't afraid of me. She was afraid of herself.

My studio is a sacred space. Those who walk in the door and have the sensitivity to feel energy, are embraced with the magic that dances all through this space. Throughout the years living and working here, I have created a safe space for spirits to inhabit. They play freely, because I invite them to run wild and inspire me to do the same. But for those who feel energy and are not comfortable with their own magic, they either shut down or turn away. It can be overwhelming.

The hour I spent with this beautiful soul showed me something about myself. It revealed just how far I'd come in my own journey of self awareness and acceptance of who I am. I used to be afraid of my own power and magic. For decades I ran from it, tried to hide it and was terrified that others would persecute me for it. I shrunk myself as small as I could manage, but no matter what I did, my own truth would not allow me to go to sleep. Not for long.

Those who have powerful souls with a purpose and mission, cannot afford to go to sleep for too long. We are needed now more than ever. But for that very reason, we are also put to the test more than most. Our evolution is on a fast track and our challenges can seem extreme. For those of us who have experienced persecution for who we are, in this lifetime or others, coming out of the shadows and exposing our truth requires that we find a way to feel safe doing so.

The tendency is to shrink, to attempt to fit in so that our differences and abilities don't cause unwanted attention. But shrinking only makes us more vulnerable. Quite the opposite is necessary. We must expand. We must fill out our bodies with the truth of our souls to such an extent that the amount of space we inhabit extends well beyond our physical form. The larger we allow ourselves to be, the safer we are to reveal who we are. And the truth is: there is nothing to fear.

Fear of being the outrageously powerful, magical being that you are is not founded in reality. Those who would silence your voice are less powerful than you are, more fearful than you are and blind to truth.

It takes some of us well into our maturity to find the courage to be who we are without apology or justification, especially if we were persecuted for it. I learned that the only way to be accepted was to fit in, but I never could. No matter how hard I tried to shrink myself, I couldn't fit. The spaces were confining and misshapen. I was fortunate. Had I fit, my soul would have shriveled and died.

The world needs us all to expand. To be who we truly are. The world needs our magic. That only happens when beautiful, powerful souls, find the courage to shine their light for all to see.

Connect With DK

www.dkhillard.com
www.dkhillardart.com
www.facebook.com/dkhillardwraptures
www.instagram.com/dkhillard
www.linkedin.com/in/debra-hillard-93526913

MONEY, POWER,
PURPOSE

Rewriting the Rules for Women Everywhere

By Timettra Wellington — Financial Literacy
Advocate, Speaker, and Entrepreneur

There's a special kind of freedom that comes when a woman learns how money works—and chooses to use that knowledge to build a life she no longer needs to escape from.

I know, because I lived it.

For years, I played by the rules society handed me. Go to school. Get a good job. Climb the ladder. But the ladder kept moving, and I found myself in a cycle so many women know too well—working hard for pennies never getting ahead. Add to that the financial aftermath of divorce. I was living for money, not with it.

Then came the shift. Not overnight, but in bold steps that required courage, curiosity, and conviction. I discovered the truth about how money really works. I uncovered real truths I had never been taught in school. That's when I made a vow: I wouldn't just break the cycle for myself. I committed myself to educating other women to do the same.

Because here's what I believe: financial independence isn't just about money. It's about choice!

When a woman understands how to make, manage, and multiply her money, she becomes powerful beyond measure. She no longer tolerates toxic workplaces or relationships out of necessity. She no longer silences her dreams for the sake of stability. She lives in her purpose, on purpose.

Yet, too many of us are still in the dark. We're smart. We're resourceful. We know how to stretch a dollar and make miracles happen. But we haven't been taught how to build generational wealth. We've been told to budget but not how to plan for life's unexpected challenges. We've been told to save but not how to grow tax-free money. We've been praised for being frugal but not taught how to create legacy.

That's why financial education is non-negotiable.

I've made it my mission to shine light on the secrets the wealthy have known for generations—how to protect your income, earn compound interest in tax-advantaged accounts, and build generational wealth with intention and strategy. I teach women how to stop living paycheck to paycheck and to start living with purpose.

Through workshops, coaching, and my work with purpose-driven women across the country, I've seen the transformation that happens when a woman takes control of her finances. Her posture changes. Her voice grows stronger. Her vision expands.

She becomes unstoppable.

This isn't a theory. This is about taking action. It's about sitting down with a financial professional who sees you. It's about asking questions, setting goals, and taking the first step, even if that step scares you. Especially if it scares you.

Ladies, we are the CEOs of our lives. Whether you're a single mom trying to make ends meet, a corporate woman ready to build your exit plan, or a retiree wondering if it's too late—it's not. The time is now!

You don't have to do it alone. If you're reading this, you've found your tribe. Link arms with me and let me help you celebrate your wins and hold you accountable. Together, we rise.

Becoming financially independent changed everything for me. But the most beautiful part? Watching other women rise with me.

You were not born to struggle.

I'll show you how to let your money work for you so you can finally walk in the fullness of who you were always meant to be.

Your future is waiting.

You are the legacy.
You are the movement.
You are unstoppable.

Connect With Timettra

www.facebook.com/timettra
www.linkedin.com/in/timettra-wellington
www.dot.cards/timettra

FREEDOM BEGINS WITHIN:

Breaking the Chains You Can't See

By Elizabeth Meigs, The Miracle Power™
Empowerment Coach & Founder of Elizabeth Inspires

You smile on the outside, but inside, something still feels off. You're showing up, doing all the *"right"* things—working hard, caring for others, holding it together—yet freedom feels like a distant dream.
You ask yourself: Why am I still stuck? Why does life still feel so heavy?

Here's the truth: many of the chains that keep us bound aren't visible. They don't rattle like iron or lock us in a cell. But they're just as real. And they quietly shape our choices, limit our dreams, and drain our strength.

Maybe for you, it's the chain of self-doubt whispering, *"You're not good enough."*
Or the chain of fear saying, *"Don't speak up. Don't risk it."*
Or maybe it's toxic stability—a life that looks secure on the outside but leaves you anxious, exhausted, and numb.

Whatever your chain is, know this:
Freedom doesn't begin after everything makes sense. Freedom begins when you dare to believe—and move—before you see the full picture.

I didn't always know that.

At 14, my world shattered when a car accident left me broken and unrecognizable. I had to relearn everything, even how to live. Years later, I entered a marriage that looked *"safe"* but slowly suffocated my spirit, confidence, and calling.

I was stuck in survival mode, and again I didn't recognize the woman I was becoming.

But in my most broken moments, I heard the voice of God whisper, *"I have a plan for you. You can't stop now."* That whisper became my lifeline. I started taking small steps of faith, even when I didn't feel strong. And what I discovered changed everything:
Belief is the first key. Movement is the second.
Even if the step is shaky. Even if you don't know where it leads.
When you choose to believe God's promises over the lies of fear...
When you take bold steps out of confusion, burnout, or bitterness...
Something shifts. The fog begins to clear. Courage rises.
And the Miracle Power™ within you comes alive.

But to keep growing—to gain the clarity and confidence to truly walk in your purpose—you have to choose to move.

This is how healing happens.

Movement, no matter how small, activates healing. It's in the decision to rise, to speak, to trust again—even before you feel ready—that your breakthrough begins.

You aren't meant to fit the mold the world demands. You have nothing to prove to anyone. And those dreams, that fire in your heart? They were placed there on purpose, for a purpose.

They're part of your assignment.

So you can't stop now. You have to keep going—if you want to fully unlock the freedom already living within you.

As Scripture says:
"Now the Lord is the Spirit, and where the Spirit of the Lord is, there is freedom." —2 Corinthians 3:17

So let me ask you:
What invisible chain are you still carrying?
What truth do you need to believe about who you are—and whose you are?
What move is God asking you to make?

This July, don't just celebrate freedom—step into it.

Ask yourself:
- What lie am I ready to release?
- What truth am I ready to believe?
- What move is God asking me to make?

If you're ready to rise into clarity, confidence, and purpose, I invite you to start tracking your transformation with my Miracle Tracker or book a complimentary Double Your PEACE Discovery Call today.

Freedom begins within. And your next step could change everything.

Connect With Elizabeth

www.elizabethinspires.com
www.elizabethinspires.com/miracle-mindset-sprint
www.facebook.com/ElizabethMeigsInspires
www.instagram.com/elizabethmeigsinspires
www.linkedin.com/in/elizabethinspires

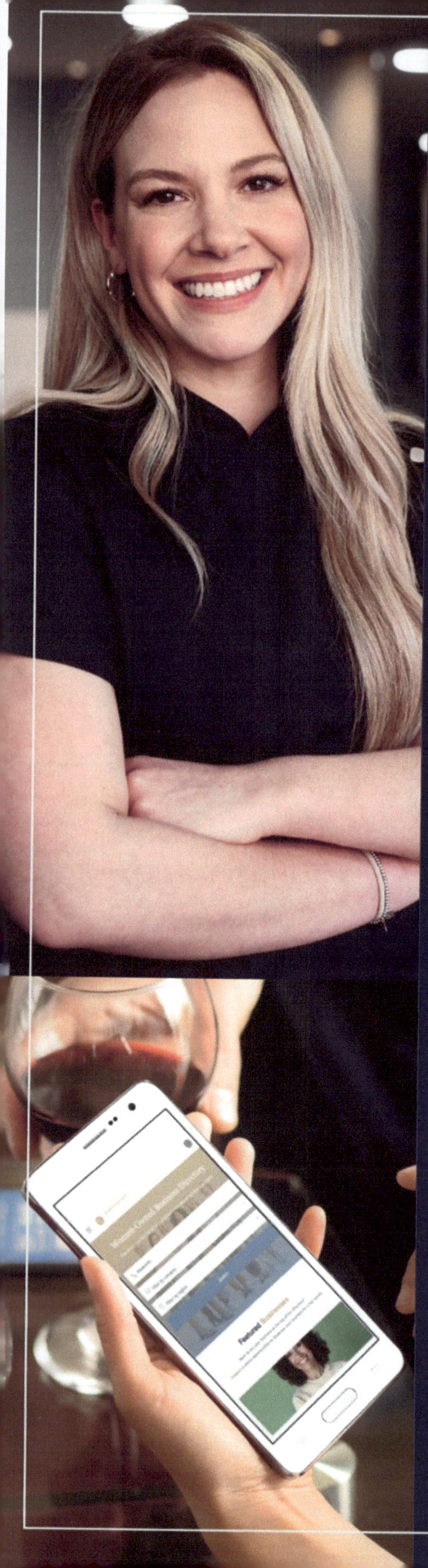

EMPOWERED
V E N T U R E S

Support women.
Discover local.
Shop with purpose.

- ☑ Discover & support women-owned businesses in every city
- ☑ Shop with purpose—locally and while you travel
- ☑ Share the power of women-owned with your network
- ☑ Join the movement—get listed, get seen, get supported
- ☑ Be the reason women-owned businesses thrive

GET LISTED
Memberships starting at $5 a month
FREE to search directory

SCAN NOW TO SIGN UP!

womenowned-business.com

Cleopatra Love Seductive

DECADENTLY GOURMAND sweet juicy cherry, nutty amaretto notes, boozy sophisticated vanilla & amber with a warm resinous note of sophistication! let's eat cake!

Cake Gourmand

Egyptian Goddess Sweet

Moonlight Mahogany Musky

Dr. Monica's Award-Winning Signature Scents
scentsually sublime

A COMPOSITION, NARRATING A STORY IN EVERY NOTE
SHOP:
DRMONICASNATURALBEAUTY.COM

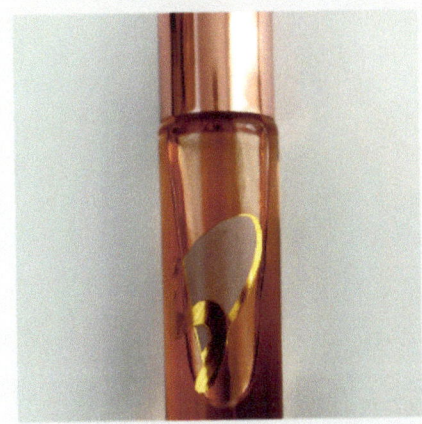

Oud Exotic Spicy

Luxe Perfume Set

Black Orchid Floral

Unapologetic Fresh

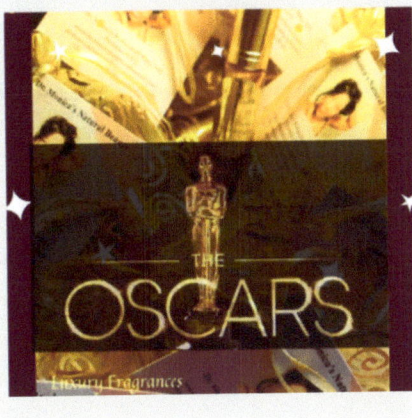

Dr. Monica Riley, MD
Founder

"Scentsually Sublime"
Luxe Natural Perfume
FRAGRANCES FROM NATURE TO

MARSAI MARTIN

Redefining Youthful Power with Confidence and Purpose

At just a young age, Marsai Martin is already a powerhouse reshaping what it means to be a confident, driven, and unapologetically authentic young woman in entertainment and beyond. As the star of Black-ish and the youngest-ever executive producer in Hollywood, Marsai is boldly breaking down barriers around age, beauty standards, and representation while using her platform to promote mental wellness and self-love. This July, The Scoop celebrates Marsai Martin in our Bold & Unapologetic edition, spotlighting her as a beacon of fearless expression and leadership.

Marsai's journey defies the typical narrative of youth in Hollywood. Far from being just a child star, she has taken control of her story by stepping behind the scenes to create content that reflects diverse experiences and empowers others to see themselves in new ways. Her business savvy and creative vision have built an empire at an age when many are still discovering their voice.

Marsai's work challenges outdated standards, proving that confidence and influence aren't tied to age or conventional beauty norms but come from authenticity and self-acceptance.

In an industry notorious for pressure and perfectionism, Marsai speaks openly about mental wellness, encouraging young people —especially young women of color—to prioritize their emotional health and embrace their uniqueness. Her advocacy is a vital part of her message, offering a fresh, relatable perspective that resonates deeply in today's culture. By sharing her own experiences with vulnerability and strength, she invites her audience to break free from limiting beliefs and celebrate their full selves.

Marsai Martin's style and presence also amplify her fearless spirit. Whether on the red carpet or in everyday life, she expresses herself with boldness, blending youthfulness with elegance in ways that challenge and expand traditional beauty standards. Her unapologetic approach to identity and self-expression is inspiring a new generation to claim their power without hesitation or compromise.

Her impact goes beyond entertainment—Marsai embodies what it means to lead with purpose, paving the way for future creators to take ownership of their narratives and cultivate spaces where diverse voices thrive. She is a role model not only for her talent but for her commitment to fostering inclusion, mental health awareness, and unapologetic self-love.

As we honor bold and unapologetic voices this July, Marsai Martin stands as a shining example of youthful empowerment. Through her confidence, creativity, and candid advocacy, she invites all women—no matter their age or background—to break free from societal expectations and live boldly, authentically, and well. Her story is a powerful reminder that true freedom is found when we rise with purpose, embrace our truth, and inspire others to do the same.

Photograph by Arnold Turner

Source: The Michigan Daily

Source: Good Morning America

NARRATIVES ROOTED IN TRUTH, DRIVEN BY RESILIENCE, AND LED BY **WOMEN**.

EMPOWER HER

HANNA OLIVAS
ALONG WITH 8 INSPIRING AUTHORS

SHOP NOW

GRAB YOUR COPY NOW

EmpowerHER: Narratives Rooted in Truth, Driven by Resilience, and Led by Women is a raw and powerful collection of real stories from women who've faced life's deepest hardships—and found strength on the other side. From illness and loss to trauma and recovery, these honest journeys reveal the power of resilience, healing, and inner transformation. More than survival, these stories show what it means to rise with purpose and lead with truth. You are not alone—and these women prove that even in the darkest moments, there is always a way forward, and always a reason to keep rising.

amazon.com　　SHE RISES STUDIOS

HELENKAGAN HEALINGARTS™

By Helen Kagan PhD

Helen Kagan PhD, an artist, scientist, psychologist, therapist, spiritual counselor and energy healer, is a creator of her unique concept HealingArts™ of 30 years integrating Art of Healing, Expressive Arts & Fine Art. Her mission-driven purpose is to deliver HealingArts™ to everyone who loves and appreciates art and will benefit from receiving healing energy from it. Her utmost intention is to introduce HealingArts to HealthCare, Residential & Hospitality Markets to assist in recovery & wellness, and to enhance healing & wellbeing.

A first-generation Russian-American, Helen brings her unique point-of-view conveying the seriousness of the current real and alternate aka "new normal" times, a sensitive Soul, not foreign to colorful abstraction of the modern Russian artistic tradition.

A bestselling Author, an *"Inspiring Woman-Leader"* by several International Magazines, a Jewish refugee from a former USSR, a pioneer in intentionally creating art for healing, Dr. Kagan continues to create her unique art to assist in healing individuals, communities, society, and the world.

"HealingArts" exhibited in multiple Galleries, Catalogs, Countries, Shows, major ArtFairs (ArtExpo, ArtBasel, RedDot, Spectrum), won awards, named *"Collectible Artist"* by many sources, is on Artsy.net and other platforms. A Bestselling Author with 5 books including co-authorship with JackCanfield and JimBritt, working on new books, has her column in 3 International Magazines. Dr. Kagan's Cover Featured in many Magazines including PassionVista as Woman-Leader(2023), International Collectors' ArtGuide (2024), Inspiring Woman-Leader, IMPAAKT(2025), Top Leaders, Magnate View(2025), Holistic Wellness Pioneers, CIOGlobal (2025). Helen's shown, published, awarded, podcasted, filmed, and is beginning her own TalkShow with BoldBrave TV, NYC.

Helen's work is simultaneously transformational, introspective, multidimensional, vibrant, and healing. She began to create her new venue Wearable HealingArts many years ago as she always wanted to bring her art to as many people as possible.

BESTSELLING AUTHORS INTERNATIONAL

Honoring Bestselling Authors Across the Globe

Dr. Helen Kagan

Since 2020, after all her big Solo Shows and Big Dreams fell apart due to pandemics, Dr. Kagan began to work on her next Big Dream and developed her new colorful creation - Wearable HealingArts® (internationally trademarked), where each designer item made from her own HealingArts, where art and healing unite in beautifully crafted high-energy garments and homeware. She's looking for sponsors and good partners specializing in Fashion Design, HealthCare & Hospitality.

Her own words:
"My mission & purpose is to encourage healing through art. In our turbulent times, amid World-wide crises, wars, fear, anxiety, stress, overwhelm & uncertainty I feel it's my duty to continue create art for healing. A severe complex PTSD survivor dedicated my life helping others, a pioneer in intentional creating art for healing, I believe in mind-body-spirit & art as a catalyst for healing individuals society & environment. I believe that now, more than ever, our World needs positive energy, spiritual intentions, gratitude, and lots of positive healing art! My passionate vibrant HealingArts called symphony of color and a vehicle for joy and well-being, is a statement of all my beliefs."

"Creating Harmony". Series Kintsugi.
Acrylic on canvas 48"x36"

This artwork embodies philosophy of finding beauty in imperfection and healing through art. It's inspired by traditional Japanese practice of Kintsugi - mending of broken pottery with gold. My *"Kintsugi"* integrates healing colors, textured surfaces, and gold-accented fissures to mimic traditional Kintsugi techniques, transforming perceived imperfections into beauty, meaning and healing.

Harmonious colors blended with golden lines evoke emotional depth, suggesting harmony is not the absence of flaws, but the integration of them into a stronger, more meaningful powerful whole. This piece invites you to reconsider the value of damage and healing, turning what was once broken into a testament of strength, beauty, and aesthetic grace.

Connect With Helen

www.HelenKagan.com
www.HelenKagan.net
www.WearableHealingArts.com
www.facebook.com/helenkagan
www.instagram.com/helenkaganarts
www.linkedin.com/in/healer

GRAB YOUR COPY NOW

Her Path to Entrepreneurship: A Journey of Courage, Vision, and Success shares the real, unfiltered stories of women who turned ambition into action—and built thriving businesses on their own terms. From startup struggles to leadership wins, these powerful journeys offer insight, strategy, and the motivation to keep going. Whether you're just beginning or growing your next big idea, this collection proves that success comes in many forms—and every path is worth celebrating. You are not alone—and these stories show that with courage and vision, anything is possible.

amazon.com   **SHE RISES**
                        STUDIOS

The *Visionary* Empowering Women, Art, and the Planet

By Hemini Mehta

In a world where glass ceilings are still being shattered and boundaries redefined, Dr Hemini Mehta stands as a luminous example of what it means to be a strong, empowered woman. British Asian, fiercely intelligent, and endlessly creative, Hemini's journey is a tapestry woven with academic excellence, entrepreneurial spirit, and a deep commitment to uplifting others—especially women—through art.

From academia to ambition, Hemini's story begins in the hallowed halls of academia. With a relentless drive for knowledge, she pursued her education all the way to a PhD, breaking stereotypes, going against the norm and inspiring countless young women along the way. But Hemini's ambitions didn't stop at scholarly achievements. She saw the world as a canvas of opportunity, and she was determined to paint her own path.

While many might rest on their academic laurels, Hemini's entrepreneurial fire led her into the world of property investment. She built a diverse portfolio, demonstrating not just business acumen but also a keen sense for nurturing and growing assets. Her property journey is more than a financial success story—it's a testament to her belief in building a legacy, creating security, and opening doors for others.

MuseScout: A Collective for Creativity
Perhaps Hemini's most inspiring venture is MuseScout, an online gallery that is far more than a marketplace—it's a thriving collective. Here, Hemini showcases her own evocative photography, but her vision extends far beyond her own lens. MuseScout is a vibrant platform where talented artists from around the globe—many of them women—are given the spotlight they deserve.

At MuseScout, every piece of art tells a story. From breathtaking landscapes captured by women photographers to bold, abstract works, the gallery is a celebration of diversity and creativity. Hemini's commitment to her artists is unwavering: 85% of every sale goes directly to the creators, empowering them to pursue their passion and sustain their craft. The remaining 15% is reinvested into discovering new talent and ensuring the artists' work reaches ever-wider audiences.

Art with a Conscience
Hemini's vision for MuseScout is rooted in sustainability. She believes that art should not only inspire, but also respects the planet. From digital prints with minimal carbon footprints to sustainable materials and local collaborations, every decision at MuseScout is made with the environment in mind. Hemini is candid about the journey: *"We're not perfect, but we are constantly trying to better ourselves."*

It's this honesty and commitment that sets her apart.

Breaking Barriers, Building Bridges
Art, for Hemini, is a universal language—one that transcends borders and breaks down barriers. She is passionate about nurturing creative talent across the globe, helping creativity flourish for the benefit of all. Her work empowers artists, supports communities, and brings extraordinary art into homes everywhere.

Hemini Mehta is more than a businesswoman or an academic—she is a force for change. Her journey is a beacon for women everywhere, proof that you can be both ambitious and compassionate, successful and sustainable.

Through MuseScout, her property ventures, and her own artistry, Hemini is helping to shape a world where women rise, creativity thrives, and the planet is cherished.

In celebrating Hemini, we celebrate the power of women to transform not just their own lives, but the world around them.

Connect With Hemini

www.musescout.com
www.instagram.com/musescout

CHANDRA DONELSON IS MAKING DATA COOL – ONE CARNIVAL AT A TIME

By Shelby Baker

When Chandra Donelson's son mistook *"data"* for a tree, she didn't laugh. She paused, and then she pivoted.

It was a fair day in every sense of the word. Donelson and her young son William were at a local carnival, walking between food stands and rides, enjoying a moment of relief in what had been a long creative struggle. Months earlier, Donelson had abandoned her passion project – a children's book about data – after what felt like her hundredth rewrite failed to pass the most important test: her son's understanding.

"I asked him what data was after reading the draft and he said, 'A tree,'" she says, recalling the moment. *"I felt like it just wasn't meant for me to do it."*

But that day at the fair, William pointed to the crowd gathered at the Ferris wheel and said, *"That's data."* And that single spark of recognition reignited everything. *"It was at that moment, I knew we had our book,"* Donelson says.

From Military Precision to Playground Conversations

Donelson's journey with data began long before storytime. A veteran of the U.S. Air Force, she's spent over a decade immersed in data analysis, eventually earning a master's degree in data science and working as a data manager for the Department of the Army.

"I've always loved solving problems, digging through the noise to find the truth," she says. *"My dad used to call me 'the little police'. I was constantly investigating things around the house and the neighborhood."*

But it wasn't until the pandemic hit that Donelson's two worlds – data and parenting – collided in a truly meaningful way.

With a laptop on the table and her son beside her, Donelson began to realize how often children are exposed to terms like data and AI without having any real understanding of them. So, she decided to do something no one else had: explain these concepts through a picture book.

Storytelling with a Side of Statistics

Creating The Data Detective at the Carnival was anything but straightforward. *"It was extremely hard,"* Donelson says. *"I wrote the book over and over again. I'd read it to William, then ask him to explain it back to me. If he couldn't, I started over."*

Each failed attempt felt like a step backward – until it wasn't.

The moment at the carnival didn't just provide clarity; it provided the entire plot. They spent the rest of the day observing games, rides, and lines, each one a hands-on lesson in data collection and critical thinking. That day became the backbone of The Data Detective, with William as both inspiration and co-creator.

"Every detail in the book is authentically him," Donelson says. *"The outfit he wears in the illustrations is one he actually owns. His bedroom in the story? That's his real room. Even the expressions on his face – we made sure everything was true to who he is."*

Representation with Intention
Donelson's vision went beyond her own child. She wanted the story to reflect the world William was growing up in: diverse, inclusive, and thoughtful.

After William saw a child in a wheelchair at the carnival, a character in a wheelchair was added to the book. *"We wanted to make sure we did as much to represent various groups,"* she recalls.

From varying skin tones to visible disabilities, the book makes representation feel natural, and it's resonating with readers.

Parents, educators, and kids alike are embracing The Data Detective, not just as a storybook but as a tool for modern education. Donelson is currently finishing a North American book tour, reaching thousands of families and championing a new kind of literacy: data literacy.

Shaping the Future of Education
For Donelson, the mission doesn't stop with one book. She's vocal about integrating data and AI into K–12 education, believing it's no longer optional.

"Until then, I will continue to spend every moment that I can teaching kids about data and AI through readings, talks, and more," she states.

To support her vision, she founded the Inspiration Library, an initiative that donates books to teachers and children in underserved communities. Through it, Donelson ensures that access to data literacy isn't limited by zip code.

An Influencer in Every Sense – Minus the Hashtags
Donelson isn't the kind of culture shaper you see trending on TikTok or modeling viral outfits on Instagram. Her influence runs deeper, built on lived experience, intellectual generosity, and radical authenticity.

She's a veteran, a mother, an entrepreneur, a storyteller, and a data evangelist all rolled into one.

And through it all, she's proving that influence isn't about selling products – it's about shifting perspectives.

It's rare to find someone who can turn analytics into a bedtime story, but Chandra Donelson makes it look easy, proving that's what happens when your brand of influence is built not on trends, but on truth.

Connect With Shelby

www.thedatadetective.org
www.instagram.com/the_data_detective
www.linkedin.com/in/chandradonelson
www.instagram.com/chandra_donelson

Mastering Risk, Growth, and Value Creation in Entrepreneurship

HER
Bold
BUSINESS MOVES

HANNA OLIVAS
ALONG WITH 16 INSPIRING AUTHORS

GRAB YOUR COPY NOW

Her Bold Business Moves: Mastering Risk, Growth, and Value Creation in Entrepreneurship is an empowering collection of stories and strategies from women who've taken bold leaps—and built thriving businesses on their terms. From embracing risk to scaling with purpose, these trailblazing entrepreneurs share how they turned challenges into opportunities and vision into impact. With practical insights and real-world lessons, this book is your roadmap to making confident moves in business and life. You are not alone— and these stories prove that boldness, backed by purpose, is the key to lasting success.

GRAB YOUR COPY NOW

She Knows Her Worth: Empowerment through Self-Respect and Confidence is a heartfelt collection of stories from women who've faced self-doubt—and found their way to unshakable confidence. Through honest reflections and practical wisdom, these women share how they built boundaries, silenced inner critics, and learned to celebrate their worth. This empowering book is both a guide and a companion for anyone ready to embrace their true value and live boldly. You are not alone—and these stories are proof that confidence grows when you choose to honor your worth, every single day.

TURNING PAIN INTO POWER THROUGH VISIBILITY

My Style, My Story, My Statement

By Katya McEwen, Founder of Oracle Cards Magic™

When the war in Ukraine began, I wasn't holding a weapon. But I was fighting to hold myself together. At the time, I was leading coaching initiatives at the top authorized telecom retailer in the U.S., working with district managers, market directors, and VPs in one of the most relentless and fast-paced industries. My role was to support leadership without letting the weight of burnout crush them. And I did it well. I had spent my life learning how to regulate in high-pressure systems that rewarded over-functioning and punished softness. It wasn't new to me. I knew how to shrink what was sacred. I knew how to show up polished and powerful, no matter what was unraveling underneath.

After that, I stepped into a coaching role at one of the top U.S. dating apps. The setting changed, but the deeper dynamic didn't.

The language was more modern, full of talk about belonging and psychological safety, but the culture still thrived on performance and productivity. On paper, I was succeeding. Inside, I felt dismembered. Fragmented between who I needed to be to fit in and who I actually was. I've always been someone who walks between worlds: Eastern and Western, corporate and spiritual, high-functioning and highly intuitive. But during that time, the war in Ukraine—my homeland—shattered whatever was holding my inner duality together. It wasn't just geopolitical trauma. It was personal disintegration. A breaking open of the compartmentalized parts I had so carefully curated.

In that raw space, I didn't reach for a strategy. I reached for symbols. I began designing Oracle cards. Not to sell.

Not to launch. Just to survive. They started as personal rituals quiet moments between grief and anger. I used AI imagery and simple words that felt like lifelines. These cards weren't created with an audience in mind. They were born out of necessity. They helped me breathe. They helped me process what I couldn't speak. Each card felt like a tiny altar, holding what my nervous system didn't have words for. Rage. Longing. Sacred memory. I wasn't building a brand. I was remembering how to stay alive.

But as I continued to create, something shifted. My survival tools became statements. And those statements began to resonate. People began asking questions. Wanting to know more. Wanting to create their own. Without realizing it, I had stumbled into the beginning of what would become Oracle Cards Magic, a community and creative platform that has now helped over 300 soulful entrepreneurs design their own decks using a blend of lived experience and AI. We've co-created more than 100 card decks. Each one a mirror. Each one a reclamation. Each one a truth made visible. This isn't just art. It's self-witnessing. It's emotional alchemy. It's what happens when people are finally given the tools to express what they've been told to hide.

I didn't start this as a business. I started it as a rebellion. A refusal to keep splitting myself between who I am and who the world expects me to be. For years, I had moved through boardrooms, coaching calls, and leadership sessions with a polished exterior that masked a deeply creative and spiritual core. I wore the fuchsia blazer into the all-beige office. I designed the card that read *"Grief is sacred"* in gold foil. I launched an intuition-based offering in an industry obsessed with data. It wasn't for attention. It was for liberation. Visibility, for me, isn't about performance. It's about integrity. It's about letting people see what I've carried, not just what I've accomplished.

Of course, not everyone understood. Some said it was just art. Some questioned the use of AI in sacred spaces. And I understand that. When you live at the intersection of multiple worlds—science and spirit, logic and emotion, neurodivergence and executive function, your truth doesn't always fit neatly into someone else's framework. But it fits in a deck. It fits in a visual. It fits in a message that says, *"This is what I've lived through. And I'm still here."*

That's the work I do now. Not because I planned to, but because the path revealed itself through grief, creation, and disruption. Just two days ago, I launched Oracle Studio, a creative community space for bold expression and identity reinvention. A place where misfits, creatives, and soul-led entrepreneurs can gather not to perform, but to remember. To make things that matter. To create not for validation, but for wholeness. The launch wasn't random. It was personal. This week marks my late brother's birthday. It's been 14 months since he passed, and I still can't believe I'm typing those words. Oracle Studio is my living tribute to him. He always told me to stop waiting. To stop hiding. To make something beautiful and bold.

I believe beauty is part of healing. Style is part of soulwork. Design is a language for identity. This is what I speak about now on stages, in interviews, on the Top 100 Powerful Women panel with Binge TV. Not because I have all the answers, but because I've chosen to live the questions out loud. The question that guides my work is this: What if visibility wasn't a performance, but a return to self?

This isn't a call to become an artist. This is an invitation to create something that lets your truth breathe. Try on the color that scares you. Write the words you've been holding back. Make the symbol for the sorrow you're still learning how to carry. Let your softness be unapologetic. Let your creative power be seen.

In a world that tells us to shrink and smile and sanitize ourselves, choosing to be visible is a radical act. And the future belongs to those who are no longer willing to perform. It belongs to the bold. The self-witnessing. The ones who show up fully. It belongs to you—if you choose it.

Connect With Katya

www.oraclecardsmagic.com
www.skool.com/oracle/about
www.facebook.com/katyamcewengorlova
www.instagram.com/katya_mcewen

By Raez Argulla
Photos by Mandi Leclaire, edited by Raez Argulla

THIS IS WHAT HAPPENED WHEN I DECIDED TO BE SEEN

How personal branding became my power move, my spiritual practice and my greatest act of self-trust

Back in late 2021, I had just quit my social media job to focus full-time on my brand photography business and to plan my wedding. I thought I'd feel free, creatively on fire, living the dream. Instead? I was tired. Stuck. Drowning in Canva carousels, blurry phone selfies, and way too many *"shoulds."*

I was promoting everything—product shoots, personal branding, lifestyle content—casting a net so wide I was practically catching air. And yet none of it felt like me in the slightest.

Post-wedding, I had time to breathe. Time to listen. And what I realized during a 2AM journal sesh when I couldn't sleep was this: it wasn't my strategy that felt off. It was my energy. I wasn't actually showing up. Not as myself, anyway.

I'd spent years managing social media for other brands, essentially cosplaying as different people online—channeling their voices, their stories, their personality. And I was good at it. But when it came time to show up for myself? Nothing. Crickets.

I realized I'd become fluent in everyone else's brand but lost my connection to my own. That hit hard.

I was furious. Mad that I'd over-delivered for others and under-recognized myself. Mad that I had real talent but had handed my power away for... applause? A paycheck? I was seething that being visible—for me—felt so damn hard.

Once the anger settled, I decided: no more. I was going to take everything I knew—branding, content, voice, visibility—and use it on myself. But it wasn't just a mindset shift. It was nervous system work. Identity work. Spiritual work.

I had to unlearn the idea that personal branding was exhausting, performative, and not meant for me. I had to get honest about how scared I was to be seen. Because once you're visible, you can't hide behind your perfectionism anymore. And that's vulnerable as hell.

So I started small.

I turned the camera on myself instead of hiding behind the graphic text slides I designed for my stories. I made silly trending Reels. I did a photo swap with another brand photographer so I could finally see myself through someone else's lens.

And guess what? People responded. In fact, they LOVED it.

Now, it's literally my job to help women step into their own spotlight. I don't just take pretty pictures. I walk my clients through a full visibility process that's part strategy, part embodiment, part hype-woman-in-your-corner energy.

Most of my clients show up to their first shoot nervous. Not sure what to wear. Unsure if they'll look *"on brand."* Terrified they'll look awkward. (Spoiler: they don't!) But after planning every detail together, with me guiding the vibe, the visuals and the energy—they show up differently.

They exhale. They soften. They start to see themselves.

And when the final gallery hits their inbox? They're not just looking at *"great photos."* They come face to face with the woman they've been becoming this whole time.

This is what visibility really is: not a performance. Not a *"hack."* It's embodiment.

It's remembering that your future self already exists. She's out there doing the thing. She's thriving, showing up, being fully seen. So you might as well start moving like her now.

You can stay small. Or you can be seen. Choose wisely.

Because every day you're silent, someone with half your talent is getting opportunities just for being louder.

You're not just the face of your brand.
You're the main character and the author!
So write your story.
And star in it.

Connect With Raez

www.raezcreative.com
www.instagram.com/raezcreative
www.linkedin.com/in/raezargulla

THE
SCOOP

PINK, PURPOSEFUL AND PROFITABLE:

Living Your Flamingo Advantage in a World of Crocs and Sharks

By Katie Hornor

When I started my first business from a dusty corner of Mexico with a baby on my hip and a vision in my heart, I didn't look like what the world told me a *"successful entrepreneur"* should be. I didn't have a business degree, a corporate background, or a sleek brand. What I had was something far more powerful: purpose.

Today, I'm an international keynote speaker, founder of The Flamingo Advantage®, and recently honored as the 2025 Visionary Coach of the Year by Insider Weekly. My books have earned multiple Book Awards. And I'm still that same woman—boldly living out my God-given purpose in full flamingo color.

Here's the truth: the world is full of crocs—copycats who blend in—and sharks—those who lead by fear, competition, or aggression. But flamingos? Flamingos stand tall. They gather in supportive communities. They are unashamed of their color. And most importantly, they live aligned with their design.

If you want to lead a business that's both purposeful and profitable, it's time to embrace your Flamingo Advantage. Here's how.

1. Show Up in Full Color

Flamingos don't ask permission to be pink. They don't apologize for standing out. How often do you dim your light to fit in with the industry norm?

Bold leadership starts with owning your uniqueness. That includes your personality, your faith, your voice, and your values. Your quirks aren't liabilities—they're your edge. When I began including flamingo metaphors into my trainings, some said it was too *"out there."* But those same metaphors are now what I'm known for. They've opened the door to stages, podcast interviews, and even a billboard in Time Square.

2. Protect Your Purpose

Flamingos often stand on one leg—not because they're quirky, but to conserve energy and allow them to stay aligned with their design. You too must protect your energy and your purpose.

That means setting boundaries around your time and attention. It means saying no to opportunities that look good but don't feel aligned. And it means anchoring your business decisions in your core mission, not the marketplace noise.

In my coaching work with successful business owners and event hosts, I see this repeatedly: the more alignement with their divine purpose and mission, the more profit follows—because their message carries conviction, not confusion.

3. Gather with the Right Flock

Flamingos thrive in flocks. And yet, too many entrepreneurs try to do business alone, or worse, they surround themselves with *"crocs"* who don't celebrate their differences.

If you're called to do business differently, you need a community that honors that. That's why I created the BOLD program—a safe space where leaders can grow without compromising their faith, family or values. Find your people. It changes everything.

4. Bold Is Better Than Big

Success isn't about being the loudest in the room—it's about being the clearest in your conviction.

When I began speaking about blending faith and business—in boardrooms, stages, podcasts, even TEDx—I wasn't the biggest name. But I was bold. That boldness has led to more visibility, trust and clients than any marketing tactic I've ever tried.

Bold doesn't mean brash or obnoxious. It means being brave enough to live intentionally and with integrity.

In a world full of crocs and sharks, your greatest advantage is being a flamingo: uniquely created, fully expressed, and faithfully aligned with your calling.

Be pink. Be purposeful. Be profitable.
And above all, be bold enough to stand in the place only you were created to fill.

Connect With Katie

www.theflamingoadvantage.com
www.youtube.com/@katiehornorflamingoadvantage
www.instagram.com/katiehornor
www.linkedin.com/in/katiehornor

UNLEARN. REWIRE. RISE.

A Guide to Shifting Paradigms and Reclaiming Freedom

By Andrea Kaye

Holy SHIFT! I did it! I made my vision a reality. This is my story. This is my message to the world.

Humanity has been stripped of our personal power and sovereignty and conditioned to give our time, energy and attention to the very systems that control us.

We've been Dumbed Down Drugged Up and Disempowered. There is a war, a spiritual battle on the mind, the manipulation of human consciousness. The powers that be understand how our minds work, how powerful we truly are and have been hindering us from reaching our true potential.

This book is a transformational guide for truth seekers or anyone ready to embody true freedom, self love and unity consciousness to transform the world. It's evident that the world needs drastic change. Within these pages is written the truth that can, will and is liberating humanity.

Just about everything I have learned over the last decade to 15 years is written within these pages. Over the last five years specifically I have studied mindset and spirituality extensively. My certifications include Akashic Records Practitioner, NLP (neurolinguistic programming), EFT (Emotional Freedom Tapping Technique), Hypnotherapy, Life and Success Coaching, Master Certification in the Alchemy is Integrative Coaching, Intuitive Healing and I am a Certified Magnetic Mind Coach doing work with neuroscience and epigenetics to rewire the brain and recode DNA. I have also decided to continue my education, at Maharishi International University, for my bachelor's in Consciousness and Human Potential.

The purpose of this book is to ignite a divine spark of remembrance within you, to awaken parts of you that have forgotten who you truly are and why you are here on this earth. For some it will be a complete dismantling of everything you thought you knew. Understand that we must unlearn and relearn to learn the TRUTH of who we are and what we are capable of.

There is a truth in this world that is kept from us to keep humanity enslaved in fear and survival giving our time, energy and attention to the very systems that are manipulating and controlling us.

My hope is that this book will awaken you to your own individual sovereignty and power so you can be part of the EVOLution rEVOLution. Truth is the power of the people is much much stronger than the people in power and love truly is the answer.

I will cover a lot in this book from the basics of quantum physics, to what mindset is and how it creates our reality, to universal law and how we can rewire our deep programmed beliefs and traumas to SHIFT our perceptions and our paradigm or the way we see and experience the world as a whole. Please keep in mind that I always encourage everyone to do their own research and form their own beliefs. Your beliefs are powerful. They create your reality. Take what resonates and leave the rest. I always say, if your beliefs are serving you well, if you are creating and living a life that you truly love or moving towards it then more power to you. If not, or if you feel there has got to be more to life than what you have been experiencing thus far, then may this book open your mind and heart to the possibility that we can create true change and transformation in the world by starting with ourselves.

My greatest hope and prayer is to be a guiding light in a world that was consumed by darkness; to show the world what is possible when we follow our dreams and live with passion and purpose walking boldly in our authenticity and truth. May we realize our beliefs are the only thing that separates us. "God" is Love, the glue that binds us. If you're ready to take the next step and turn awareness into lasting transformation, I invite you to visit my *https://linktr.ee/miraclemaven*

Here you'll find the book and a range of services designed to support your continued awakening, healing, and empowerment including Holistic Health and Wellness Products, Quantum Healing Technology and State of the Art Magnetic Mind Coaching for Total Wellness and Transformation Mind Body & Spirit.

Let's explore what path forward best supports you in living fully aligned with your highest truth & greatest potential.

The shift has begun. Now let's make it real. Together we can create the New Earth. Make Shift Happen. Let's GROW.

Available NOW   Amazon Ebook Links for Dumbed Down Drugged Up & Disempowered

Connect With Andrea

www.Facebook.com/andrea.shive
www.YouTube.com/@conspiracyrealistyouniverse

Where Ambitious Women Launch & Scale with Confidence

Your go-to platform for e-commerce resources, business strategy, and confidence-boosting money management.

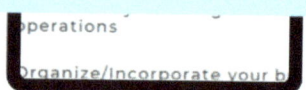

Grab the FREE 10-Step Business Checklist!

What We Offer

- Business mentoring for ecommerce & digital product startups
- Money management systems designed for you to be the CEO of your life
- Self-paced resources that teach you to build, grow, and own your success
- Tools that teach — not just tell you what to do

Who We Help
Women ready to turn their dreams into revenue-generating businesses.

Ready to Build a Business You Love?
www.empowerher.ventures
www.empowerher.ventures/free-checklist
www.instagram.com/empowerherventures
www.facebook.com/empowerherventures
www.Linkedin.com/company/102082847

Personalized & Flexible Education For Grades K-8

IAOMAI ACADEMY
Unlocking Potential and Inspiring Confidence

Big Potential, Small Setting - Where Bright Minds Thrive

ABOUT US

Iaomai Academy is a K–8 microschool located in Fredericksburg, Virginia, dedicated to supporting bright students with diverse learning needs in a small, nurturing setting where they can thrive. Our program is designed for families who are currently homeschooling or seeking a more personalized educational path—one that fosters confidence, curiosity, and a renewed love for learning. Our model has successfully helped students improve by two or more grades in one academic year!

WHY CHOOSE US

Self-paced learning to enable mastery of concepts

Learning coaches to provide small group and 1:1 support for each child

Flexible enrollment options - attend 2 or 3 days a week

APPLY TODAY!

Follow us on Facebook and Instagram @iaomaiacademy

CONTACT US

Visit: www.iaomaiacademy.com
Email: info@iaomaiacademy.com
Call: (540) 227-3904
Fredericksburg, VA 22408

The SHE RISES STUDIOS PODCAST

TUNE IN. RISE UP. THRIVE.

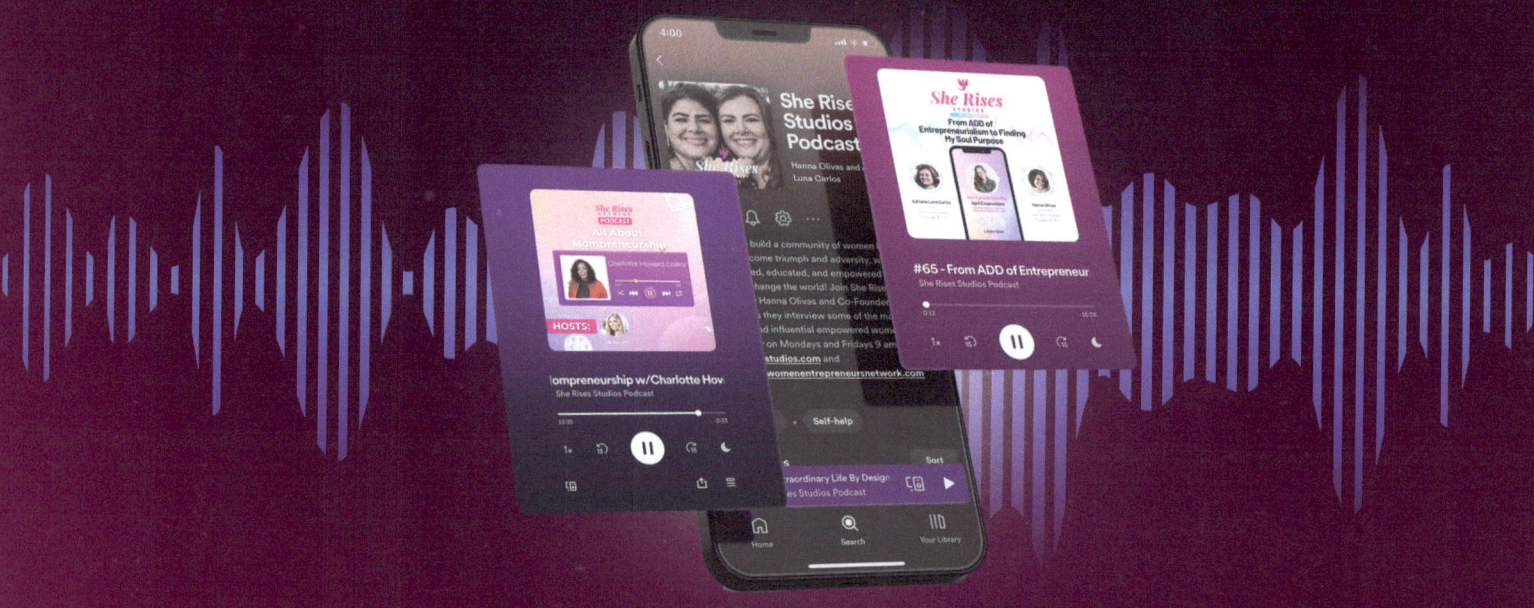

Looking for **real conversations** that inspire, empower, and ignite your potential? The **SRS Podcast** is where women like you come to **learn, grow, and rise!**

Join us for powerful **interviews with trailblazing entrepreneurs, thought leaders, and everyday women** who have turned obstacles into opportunities. Our episodes dive into:

➢ **Breaking through self-doubt** and stepping into confidence
➢ **Building a thriving business** with purpose and passion
➢ **Mastering work-life balance** without guilt
➢ **Leveling up your mindset, health, and career**
➢ **Finding your true purpose and living boldly**

Each episode is packed with **real stories, expert insights, and actionable strategies** to help you take your life to the next level. **This isn't just a podcast—it's your roadmap to success!**

SUBSCRIBE NOW AND START YOUR JOURNEY TO EMPOWERMENT!

SHE RISES
S T U D I O S

JOIN THE SRS COMMUNITY

WHERE WOMEN RISE TOGETHER!

Connect. Empower. Thrive. Whether you're an entrepreneur, professional, or simply seeking inspiration, **this is your space to grow!**

- Daily Motivation
- Expert Insights
- Sisterhood & Support

You don't have to do it alone—let's rise together!

JOIN NOW!

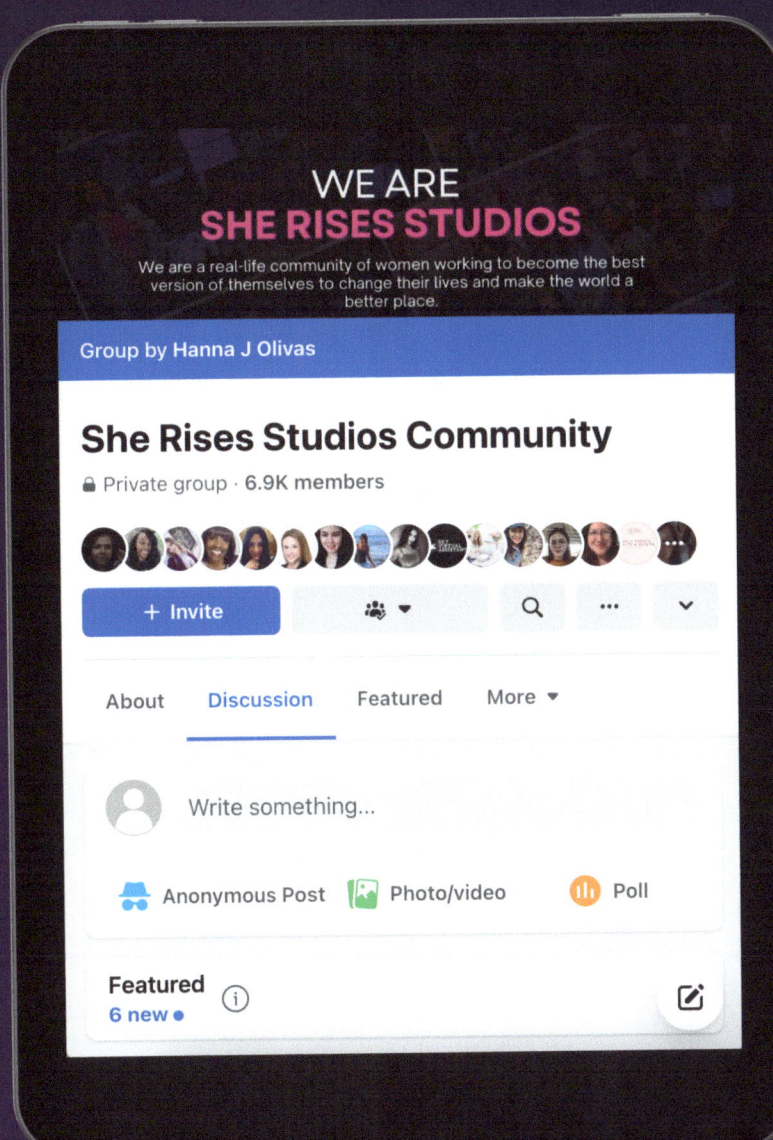

www.bit.ly/srscommunitygroup   www.sherisesstudios.com

LAKEITH STANFIELD:

Breaking Molds Through Fearless Art and Fashion

LaKeith Stanfield is a name that reverberates with fearless creativity, unapologetic self-expression, and a relentless challenge to societal norms. In a culture that often rewards conformity, LaKeith has built a career and public identity rooted in breaking molds—whether through the complex characters he portrays or his distinctive, boundary-pushing fashion choices. As we celebrate Bold & Unapologetic: The Era of Fearless Expression this July, The Scoop honors LaKeith Stanfield, an artist whose work and style are vivid declarations of freedom, vulnerability, and authenticity.

From the moment he stepped into the spotlight, LaKeith made it clear that he would not be confined by traditional Hollywood archetypes. His breakthrough role in Short Term 12 showcased his ability to convey intense emotional depth, while films like Get Out and Sorry to Bother You allowed him to explore socially charged narratives that question systemic oppression and identity politics. LaKeith chooses roles that challenge audiences and disrupt comfortable narratives. Rather than accepting typecasting, he builds characters layered with complexity, often reflecting the nuances of marginalized experiences.

His portrayal of Fred Hampton in Judas and the Black Messiah earned critical acclaim, not just for its raw power but for the way it captured the vulnerability and humanity of a revolutionary leader.

This commitment to authenticity extends beyond his performances. LaKeith's fashion sense has become a powerful tool of self-expression, as he uses style to question and expand ideas of gender, beauty, and identity. On red carpets and in everyday life, he embraces bold, avant-garde looks that mix fluidity with sharp tailoring, flamboyance with subtlety. His fearless approach to fashion challenges rigid definitions of masculinity and dares others to rethink how clothing can be a form of storytelling and liberation. By blending elements from different aesthetics and eras, LaKeith creates a unique visual language that defies easy categorization. He makes it clear that fashion is not about fitting in but about standing out and owning your truth.

LaKeith's impact is deeply tied to his willingness to be vulnerable in public spaces. In interviews and social media, he has spoken openly about mental health, the pressures of fame, and the journey to self-acceptance. He resists the expectation that artists, especially Black men, must project invulnerability. Instead, he models a new kind of strength—one that embraces complexity, emotions, and the messiness of growth. This vulnerability not only humanizes him but also creates space for his audience to feel less alone in their struggles.

Source: GQ

Photograph by Micaiah Carter

LaKeith's openness about his personal challenges and reflections encourages others to find freedom in their own stories, breaking the silence around mental health and identity.

LaKeith Stanfield also embodies a broader cultural shift—one where creative freedom is intertwined with social consciousness. His projects and public persona engage with pressing issues of race, class, and representation, making his work both personally resonant and culturally significant. He does not separate art from activism; rather, he uses his platform to uplift marginalized voices and challenge systemic inequities. This fusion of creativity and advocacy makes his contributions especially vital in today's digital and social climate, where visibility and narrative control are powerful tools for change.

As the landscape of entertainment and fashion evolves, LaKeith stands at the forefront of a movement redefining what it means to be a modern artist. He proves that success does not require sacrificing identity or compromising authenticity. Instead, it calls for courage—the courage to express your truth boldly, to embrace your vulnerabilities, and to invite others into a conversation about freedom that is as complex as it is necessary.

In celebrating LaKeith Stanfield this July, The Scoop acknowledges not only his artistic talents but his role as a trailblazer in fearless expression. His journey is a powerful reminder that breaking molds is not just about being different for difference's sake. It is about creating space for fuller, richer, and more honest human experiences. LaKeith's art and style inspire us to claim our own freedom—to live unapologetically and to let our truest selves shine.

In the era of bold and unapologetic expression, LaKeith Stanfield is more than an actor or fashion icon. He is a revolutionary voice, using every medium at his disposal to reshape culture and remind us that authentic expression is a profound act of liberation.

THE BEAUTY OF PURPOSE:

Dr. Chanell Dingle-Sermon's Royal Mission of Impact

Dr. Chanell Dingle-Sermon, the first reigning Ms. Southern States United Crown of America, is a true trailblazer in education, ministry, and pageantry. She is an award-winning educator, pastor, and nonprofit CEO who has held pageant titles on state, national, and international levels. She graduated with a 4.0 G.P.A. from Capella University, obtaining a Doctor of Education degree in Curriculum and Instruction. Dr. Sermon's mission in education, ministry, and pageantry is framed in three words: edify, exhort, and empower as it relates to impacting the lives of others. She uses the painful lessons from her life experiences to bring hope to others who are confronted with the same or similar issues. Struggles with confidence, esteem, and self-worth resulting from family dysfunction, bullying, and being constantly ridiculed during her early years, interfered with her ability to enjoy life as a young adult. However, after removing herself from the environments that kept breaking her, she learned and discovered so much more about herself that allowed her to become a catalyst for uplifting others in all that she does. As the three-time recipient of the I AM H.E.R. International *"Teacher of the Year"* award and a two-time recipient of the I AM H.E.R. International S.T.E.A.M. Award, she has dedicated her career to modeling what an effective arts education should look like in the classroom to show why the arts should be kept in schools as it affects the livelihood of teachers of the arts, students of the arts, and societal consumers of the arts. As a pastor and theologian recognized with international honorary doctorates in divinity and philosophy from the Mount Olives Ministerial Bible Institute, she provides practical, faith-based strategies to maintain, improve, and achieve mental wellness on her YouTube channel, Pretty Doc Ministries. Additionally, she established a national nonprofit organization, Kappa Epsilon Lambda Royal Christian Sorority, Incorporated as a safe haven for Christian women to celebrate sisterly love in Christ while corporately serving others in their communities. And finally, as a trailblazing pageant queen, she has creatively and exceptionally aligned with the vision of every platform that she represents. This includes combining her experiences as a teacher and ministry leader to connect beauty to life and learning through serving others in her region. Today, Dr. Sermon continues to deliver faith-based content online and in-person to heal and uplift communities around her.

Connect With Dr. Chanell

www.iamprettydoc.com
www.mssouthernstates.yourwebsitespace.com/
www.youtube.com/@prettydocministries
www.facebook.com/share/16V6NyH1Vc/?mibextid=wwXlfr
Instagram: @iamprettydoc

AMBER KRYSTAL:

A Voice for Healing, Wholeness and Maturity

Amber Krystal is a dynamic faith leader, speaker, and spiritual mentor known for her bold message of healing, wholeness, and maturity. As the founder of HWMM Ministries and the visionary behind Be Healed. Be Whole. Be Mature: A Place of Metamorphosis, Amber has committed her life to guiding people through the life-changing journey of personal and spiritual transformation.

Affectionately called The Female Moses, Amber walks in a prophetic mandate to lead others out of the bondage of past trauma, fear, and religious legalism into a life of authentic freedom and divine purpose. Her ministry was birthed from a deeply personal wilderness season, where God revealed to her the necessity of inner healing before destiny could be fulfilled. Amber teaches that true confidence, leadership, and influence are rooted in transparency, spiritual maturity, and a healed heart.

Her bold, unfiltered message has opened doors across both ministry and marketplace platforms. Amber has been featured in AP News, Yahoo Global Media, Google News, Paramount films, and Hallmark movies and holds an IMDb credit for her work in the entertainment industry. A published writer and rising media personality, she recently graced the cover of Neuworldz Magazine, a digital magazine with over 1M viewers, sharing her heart for women navigating transformation and healing.

Amber's powerful voice reached global audiences when she took the TEDx stage, boldly declaring the importance of confronting brokenness to access destiny. Her talk, much like her ministry, challenged conventional mindsets and inspired a movement of people determined to embrace their metamorphosis.

Her latest book, A Call to the Wilderness: A Pursuit to Purpose and Destiny, captures the prophetic insight and hard-earned wisdom gleaned from her own spiritual journey. In it, Amber shares how seasons of isolation and pruning are often divine setups for extraordinary purpose.

Through her syndicated podcast, speaking engagements, and growing online ministry, Amber Krystal continues to lead a new generation of believers toward healing, identity, and bold spiritual maturity. Her life and message serve as a reminder that transformation isn't a suggestion — it's a requirement for those destined to impact the world.

Connect With Amber

www.hwmministries.com
Instagram: @iamamberkrystal
Facebook: Amber Krystal

she♥wins

WOMEN'S NETWORK

Elevate your business with the power of community.

Get access to the tools, connections, and support you need to grow—with a circle of women who truly get it.

WHAT'S INCLUDED

- Strategic networking & mentorship
- Expert-led masterclasses & exclusive resources
- Member spotlights, VIP perks & more

Join for just

$87/MONTH

no contracts, cancel anytime.

www.shewinswomensnetwork.com

SHE RISES
S T U D I O S

*U*NLEASH YOUR STORY

BECOME A PUBLISHED AUTHOR!

Have you ever dreamed of sharing your wisdom, experience, or passion with the world? **Now is your time!**

Publishing a book isn't just about writing—it's about **establishing your authority, inspiring others, and creating a lasting legac**y. Plus, with the **$138.5 billion book industry** booming, there's never been a better moment to step into the spotlight.

At **SRS Publishing**, we don't just publish books—we **elevate voices, empower authors, and create change-makers**. Our mission is to help women break barriers, amplify their stories, and thrive in the publishing world. Whether you're an entrepreneur, thought leader, or storyteller at heart, **we're here to guide you every step of the way.**

JOIN THE FASTEST-GROWING PUBLISHING HOUSE FOR WOMEN IN THE USA.

READY TO TURN YOUR DREAM INTO REALITY?

www.SheRisesStudios.com | contact@sherisesstudios.com

CONFIDENCE IN ACTION:

How *Gina Redzanic* Is Helping Others Stand Tall And Lead Boldly

Confidence isn't just a buzzword—it's a way of being. And no one embodies that truth more powerfully than Gina Redzanic, a Self-Confidence Coach, Business Educator, and Best-Selling Author who has made it her life's work to help others rise into their worth. Whether she's mentoring a teen battling insecurity or guiding an entrepreneur through self-doubt and visibility fears, Gina shows up with clarity, compassion, and a strategy for real, lasting transformation.

With a professional foundation built on small business ownership, direct sales, affiliate marketing, and certified coaching through Maxwell Leadership, Gina's journey is one of both heart and hustle. Her story isn't about overnight success or curated perfection—it's about growth through intention, resilience, and a deep desire to serve.

"I believe everyone deserves to feel confident, capable, and worthy," Gina says. *"Confidence isn't something you're born with—it's something you build. It's a skill, and with the right support and mindset, anyone can learn to stand in their power."*

That philosophy is at the core of everything she does. Through personalized coaching, impactful workshops, speaking engagements, and her bestselling book, Gina has touched lives across industries, generations, and backgrounds. Her clients range from emerging teen leaders to seasoned business professionals, all seeking the same thing: the freedom to show up fully and unapologetically.

Coaching with Heart—and Results

Gina's coaching style is refreshingly direct, deeply empathetic, and highly results-oriented. She doesn't just offer inspiration—she provides a roadmap. Drawing from the powerful leadership principles of the Maxwell framework, Gina helps her clients identify and dismantle limiting beliefs, set aligned goals, and take bold action that sticks.

Her clients often come to her feeling stuck or overwhelmed, wrestling with imposter syndrome or lacking direction. *"So many people believe they're not good enough, that they don't belong in the room, or that someone else is more qualified,"* she explains. *"I help them rewrite that story. We replace fear with clarity and self-doubt with strategy."*

That blend of mindset and method is what sets Gina apart. She understands that success isn't just about doing more—it's about becoming more self-aware, more intentional, and more aligned with your purpose.

Empowering the Next Generation

While Gina is a force in the business world, her work with teens is equally close to her heart. Through mentorship programs, one-on-one coaching, and youth workshops, she helps young people develop the self-worth and emotional intelligence that many don't encounter until much later in life.

"I wish I had someone pouring into me as a teen, helping me believe in myself and see my value," Gina shares. *"That's why I do this work. Teens face so much pressure, and confidence becomes the foundation for making healthy choices, cultivating strong relationships, and stepping into leadership."*

In a world filled with comparison and constant digital noise, Gina's message to young people is both grounding and empowering: You are already enough. Now let's build on that.

A Voice That Resonates

Beyond the coaching space, Gina is a sought-after speaker, podcast guest, and writer. Her voice has become synonymous with confidence, clarity, and courage. Whether she's sharing on stage or contributing to conversations online, her words cut through the noise and connect with authenticity.

Her bestselling book (title withheld in this version) is a testament to her commitment to helping people tap into their inner strength. In it, she weaves personal stories, coaching tools, and mindset shifts that challenge readers to rise above fear and embrace who they truly are.

Audiences and readers alike appreciate her real-talk approach—no fluff, just powerful insights that prompt reflection and action.

Leading by Example

In her own life, Gina practices what she preaches. She stays grounded by prioritizing her family, including her husband, two daughters, and their beloved dogs. She embraces movement and balance through fitness classes, and she carves out space for fun, connection, and growth in all areas of life.

"I believe in being present for my people and my purpose," she says. *"That's where confidence grows—in showing up fully in your own life."*

This commitment to alignment and authenticity is what makes Gina not just a coach, but a leader in every sense of the word. She's not just helping people dream bigger—she's walking beside them as they turn those dreams into reality.

What's Next

Looking ahead, Gina is expanding her reach through new programs, teen mentorship initiatives, and additional writing projects. She's also building more opportunities to collaborate with schools, organizations, and women-led businesses who want to empower their teams from the inside out.

Whether she's working one-on-one or speaking to a room full of leaders, her mission remains the same: to help people believe in themselves, lead with confidence, and create lives that reflect their deepest truth.

"Confidence isn't about being loud or perfect," Gina says. *"It's about knowing who you are, standing in your truth, and showing up with purpose. That's what I want to model. That's what I want to help others build."*

In a world that often tells us to play small or stay quiet, Gina Redzanic is a powerful reminder that we're allowed to rise—and that the journey to confidence is one worth taking, together.

Connect With Gina

www.facebook.com/gina.pantanoredzanic
www.instagram.com/the.self.confidence.coach
www.linkedin.com/in/gina-redzanic

SPEAK AT SHE WINS GLOBAL SUMMIT 2025

NOVEMBER 6–7, 2025 | LAS VEGAS, NV

The **She Wins Global Summit 2025** is calling all bold, passionate, and purpose-driven women to take the stage. This powerful **2-day event** will bring together over **500 women leaders, entrepreneurs, and professionals** from around the world for a transformational experience. As a speaker, you'll share your knowledge, story, or expertise in front of a **global audience**—while gaining massive visibility, media exposure, and high-level networking opportunities.

Topics include finance, leadership, business growth, mental health, branding, AI, wellness, innovation, diversity, public speaking, and more. Speaker benefits include a premier speaking slot, TV broadcast of your talk on FENIX TV, media features, red carpet experience, a premium swag bag, gourmet lunch for both days, custom promo graphics, and two full event passes—**valued at over $2,000**, all included with your speaker package.

If you're ready to lead, inspire, and make a real impact, this is your moment. Share your voice, elevate your brand, and join a global movement of unstoppable women.

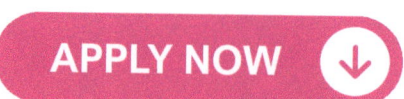

APPLY NOW

 https://form.jotform.com/250646617740156

GET YOUR COPY NOW

Celebrate the power of women through inspiring stories and insights.

The Unimaginable Journey
Beth MacGowan

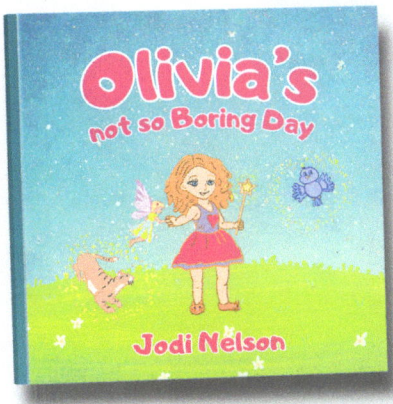

Olivia's Not So Boring Day
Jodi Nelson

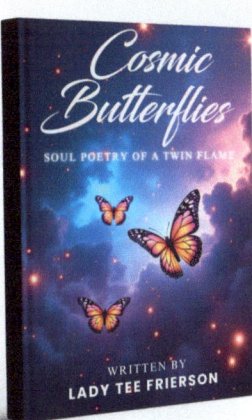

Cosmic Butterflies
Tymquana Frierson

The Christmas Wreath
Dr.Dawn Menge

Dreaming with My Eyes Open
Michela Perry

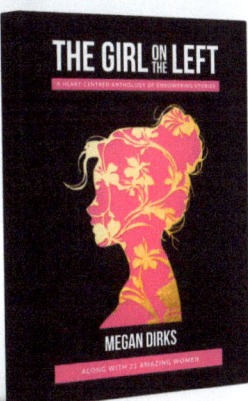

The Girl on the Left
Megan Dirks

A Certain Kind of Sadness
Jillean McClory

Cruz Control
Melissa Cruz

Retreat Within Me
Hoda Jaludi